THROUGH THE PAIN

Through the Pain

Jacqueline Allen

Superior Publishing LLC.

Contents

Rest In Peace...		vii
references		ix
1	I Am Jacqueline Allen	1
2	Sexual Abuse	4
3	Physical Abuse	8
4	Don't Worry	11
5	Hurt People	13
6	Emotional, Physical & Mental Abuse	17
7	Encouragment and Inspiration	22
8	So-Called Friends & True Friends	27
9	Prison Set Me Free	31
10	Pain on Top of Pain	36
11	Can't Do it Alone	39
12	Dealing with Pain through God's Word	41
Just To Say Thanks		43

Copyright © 2021 by Jacqueline Allen

All rights reserved. No part of this book may be reproduced in any manner whatsoever without written permission except in the case of brief quotations embodied in critical articles and reviews.

Superior Publishing, 2021

My biggest supporters, they are gone but not forgotten. Their words will live with me forever.
Martha N. Bean, Jimmie D. Holland, Maria Taylor,
Annie M. Pierce and James Pierce.

King James Version
New International Version
Footprints in the Sand, Author Margaret Fishback Powers

1

I Am Jacqueline Allen

I remember when I was a little girl back in 1982, growing up on a hog farm right off the Highway going toward West Point, MS. There I was, in a small town called Prairie. I remember just like it was yesterday, because this is when I first met pain. But before I go into my pain let me introduce myself.

My name is Jacqueline Allen I was born in Houston, MS to Mr. James and Mrs. Annie Pierce. I am the oldest of five children. I am the mother of three sons, and I have eight grandchildren. I was raised in Okolona, Mississippi. I joined Red Bud Missionary Baptist Church at an early age. Growing up in my house there was no such thing as not going to church. We were made to go no excuses.

Growing up around the Godly women that I had in my life I always heard of God. They always talked about His goodness and mercy and they knew because of their experiences and their faith that everything was going to be alright.

Getting older I found out that there is a difference in hearing about God and getting to know Him for yourself.

Knowing about God comes from hearing what others have said about Him.

Knowing God comes from the experiences that you have gone through or the things that have happened in your life. These things were the things that made us call out to Him, knowing that He was the only One that could help and save you. And in times like these, is when we come to know Him in a real personal way. There is no greater feeling that you will have than when you get to know God for yourself.

It was through the pains in my life that I came to know Jesus in a personal way. Hebrews 13:5-6 God said, never will He leave me, never will He forsake me."

There are many kinds of pains that a person could face in this life. I have discovered that Jesus has an answer for all of them.

There is physical, emotional, mental, and spiritual pain. There is no one on earth that can heal your pain like Jesus. The pains that we deal with is not supposed to break us, but to make us stronger and bring us into a closer relationship with God.

In this book we are going to look at some of that pains that I faced in my daily life and the answers that God gave me, and prayerfully they will help you deal with the pain that you are facing.

We have to remember that "There's no healing if there's no pain. There's no rainbow without the rain."

Physical pain is what most people refer to when something hurts. Physical pain can be caused by many things.

Emotional Pains are when we are holding on to things that we should let go of.

Mental Pain is an unpleasant feeling. Mental pain is intense and feels unbearable.

Spiritual Pain, I feel like, comes from being lost separated from God.

In John 16:33, KJV I have said these things to you, that in me you may have peace. In the world you will have tribulation, but take heart, I have overcome the world."

Through the pain was inspired by the pain I have endured over the years. It was through the pain that I found myself healing and come to know God for myself in a real and a personal way.

It's pain being lost in the world, standing at the crossroads of life and not knowing which way to go.

The pain that I experienced kept me bound and made me bitter and full of resentment. Resentment that eventually led me to prison, but it was there in prison that I was able to deal with my pain. And it was there in prison that I experienced God's divine healing. No matter what you face in life, I just want to encourage you to never give up on God and never give up on yourself.

My 3 P's are what helped me to get through and they are:
PRAY, PRAISE AND PUSH! JESUS WINS OVER ALL!

2

Sexual Abuse

    1982, a year I will never forget, growing up on a hog farm right off the highway going towards West Point. Here I was just a little girl in a little town called Prairie, about to make an entrance to a life of pain.

    I remember that night like it was last night, my mom and stepdad had been drinking and my mom told me to go to bed. Over in the night, my stepdad came and got in bed with me and I told him he was in the wrong room. I yelled, as if it were a fire in the house, yelling for my mom, but she had drunk so much she never heard me, she never came. I was able to fight him off that night, little did I know this was just the beginning of beginnings.

    The next morning, I told my mom what had happened. After she talked to him, my stepdad, she said that I should not be spreading lies like that. I felt so hurt, hearing her say that to me, felt even more worse than what my stepdad had tried to do. She did not believe me! My mom did not believe me! She was supposed to protect me! It made me angry with her, so I rebelled against her. I told my uncle what had happened, but then after a while it happened again, but this time I had tried to hide when they started drinking, but my mom found me and told me to go to bed. I got into bed, but I was so scared I could not sleep. When I finally fell asleep, I was awakened by my door opening. It was him! I started looking for something to protect myself, but my mom popped up. She saw him and asked what he was doing. Of course, he lied and said he was going to the bathroom. But they had their own bathroom at the other end of the house. I pointed that out to my mom but then, my stepdad said their bathroom was broken. So once again, my mom took his side. My anger was explosive, it went through the roof. I could no longer control myself; I did not even know how to control my anger anymore. I started breaking things in the house, throwing things at my mom and her husband! I just wanted to hurt them both.

    After that, I started telling my mom every time he came near me, he stopped supporting me. So, I ended up at the age of twelve doing things that no child should have to do in order to get the things that they need.

    I began to let men and boys touch me and it made me feel so dirty and so broken on the inside. I started to smoke and drink, I wanted to bury the pain, like dogs bury bones. I wanted this to go away. I stayed away from home with whoever would let me stay with them, cousins or friends. It did not matter, I had to get away.

    After a while, I started missing my mom, so I went back home. At first, everything was good. I stayed away from my stepdad, and in turn he avoided me as well. But it was not long, the partying and drinking started again. My heart dropped to the bottom of my stomach. I went to my room and got into bed, I fell asleep, only to be awaken by my stepdad, he was rubbing on me, I saw that he was naked, I was sick! And I was angry! I knew telling my mom would not do any good. I did not bother to call out to her anymore, so I stabbed my stepdad with a fork on his private part. I told him he better no touch me ever again! I just knew after this that everything would come to the light. I knew without a doubt my mom would believe me this time, because I had evidence, I could tell her what I did, how I fought him off. I called my uncle and asked him to come, so that I could tell him and my mother what had happened, but my mom said she had done that to my stepdad years ago. My heart and mouth dropped. I ran out of that house and never looked back that broke me all the way down.

I made a vow to protect all the other young ladies that ever had to face what I did. I always want to be a listening ear because I had no one to listen to me.

I left home at the age of fourteen and stayed wherever I could with friends, family even with people that I did not even know as long as they were nice to me.

My mom found me and took me to court and tried to make me come home, but I was sixteen and pregnant and when I told the judge why I left home he did not order me to go back. That was a happy day. God came through on time.

Life's challenges and obstacles can cause us to feel overwhelmed with heartaches, sadness and despair. These are times that it is vital that we draw closer to God. God is our Father, Our All-Knowing Father, He knew what we would encounter before the foundation of the earth was laid. He already knew what I was going to face before I was even created. He had already set up an internal encouraging system within us to assist us during difficult times. It is when you accept Jesus as your personal Savior then you have a great Protector in your corner.

No means no and that should be that! Grown men should understand that and leave these little girls alone! Just know that there day is coming!

Before I was able to forgive my stepfather, I had to learn to forgive myself. Before my stepfather died, he called me to come and see him. I only went to tell him that I forgave him but before I could say anything, he apologized to me. I let him know that I had already forgiven him.

Matthew 6:14-15 For if ye forgive men their trespasses, your Heavenly Father will also forgive you.

3

Physical Abuse

1985, at the age of seventeen, all alone with a little a baby I really felt lost. I started using my body to get the things that I needed for me and my son. I still thank God to this day that I never caught a disease.

Finally, my son's father stepped up and helped me get an apartment. Later, I found a job and things started to look up for me. I was finally happy! Well at least I thought.

After getting set up in my new home I decided to let my son's father move in with us. At first, everything was great! But then, the beating began. I began blaming myself. I tried to make sure that I did everything right, trying to please him so that he would not want to jump on me but nothing I did was right. He stayed mad all the time. Everything I did was wrong, everything I said was wrong. He would invite friends over and if one of them looked at me he would hit me saying I was flirting with his friends. He made me feel like I couldn't cook or clean and this always led to a fight. I was tired of all the fighting. He promised me that he would not hit me again. I believed him and I forgave him. Time had passed and everything was still good.

One night he did not come so I called his mom because I was worried about him. I was afraid something had happened to him. But when he made it home, he jumped on me and told me that I was not to be out looking for him. He went on to say that he knew where home was and he knew when he wanted to be there. He said some of his friends had told him that they saw me out walking around with the baby looking for him. I told him that was a lie! The only thing I did was call his mom. I could not take any more! I had had enough! I began to pack my stuff. He pleaded with me, begging me to stay, saying how sorry he was, he even promised me that he would never hit me again. I forgave him again at that moment, but my mind was made up, I was still going to leave soon.

I got a call that one of my cousins had been killed, so I had a family member to come and pick me up so that I could be with them. My son's dad called me and I told him what was going on and where I was, he was okay with that, he told me to just take my time. I hang up knowing that everything was okay between us. When I got home we sat and talked and got into bed. I was awaken to him beating me, saying that I had no respect for him as a man and he was tired of it! He wasn't the only one tired, I was tired and everything in me knew that this was the last time he would ever put his hands on me. I got on my knees and I cried out to the Lord, "Lord Lord help me please!" The next day I went to the store and ran in to a childhood friend, we begin to talk and I began to cry, telling her about my situation and the things that I was going through. And check God out, I was in the right place at the right time! She said that she had an apartment for me and my son! That night, I went to sleep praising and thanking God. God had done it again, He stepped in right on time! When my son's daddy left for work the next morning, my son and I left that house and never looked back. He found us about two weeks later, and tried to make me come home, but the answer was NO! I took a beating but it set me free.

I found myself wanting peace in my life. I was growing, I was maturing and it felt so good. I left Aberdeen and went to Shannon. God gives timely instructions that not only affect and benefit us, but others who know us and also those that have no clue who we are. When God tells us to do something, it is wise to be obedient because there is a purpose in His timing and plan. I discovered there is power in being obedient. As you journey through life one day at a time, don't discount the instructions God has for your life.

There is a purpose in God's plan. And if you love God you will obey all that He has commanded you to do. Act when and how the Lord commands you to act. Follow God's timely instructions and watch how God comes through for you. Joshua 2, John 14:15 and John 14:21-26.

When you can see others as God sees them you will learn to love them like God loves them. My sons' father and I are now the best of friends.

4

Don't Worry

God is never blind to our tears, never deaf to our prayers and never silent to our pain.

He sees, He hears and He will deliver! If we let God use us He promises 3 things, taking a look at Joshua.

First, God promises strength. No one will be able to stand against you. Joshua1:5 Whatever God asks you to do He'll give you the power to do it.

Secondly, God promises success. You will be successful. Joshua 1:6 God wants you to succeed in serving Him. He doesn't want you to be a failure.

Thirdly, God promises support. I will be with you where ever you go. Joshua 1:19 God's word is done. God's way will not lack God's support. Joshua 1:8 says always remember what is written in this book. Study it day and night to be sure to obey everything that is written there. If you do this, you will be wise and successful in everything.

God promises of success is not based on our ability. It is based on our commitment of His Word. Ephesians 3:20 Now unto Him that is able to do exceedingly abundantly above all that we ask or think, according to the power that worketh in us.

Joshua 1:5 God will be with us and He will.

5

Hurt People

    I have learned in life that hurt people hurt other people because they want others to feel the pain that they feel or felt. Maybe they had no one to talk to or no one to comfort them or maybe they felt all alone with no one to turn to.
    Some people because they had no one to share their pain with, began sharing with alcohol. They started drinking and doing drugs whatever they can do to ease their pain. They have even vented to others. I have had people to tell me that I don't know why you are smiling and so happy. At the time of the question, I didn't have an answer, because I really didn't know myself. But what I did know is that I didn't want any little girl to suffer the things that I did all of the abuse that I dealt with and went through. But I did tell them about how Jesus rescued me and how I was able to walk away and not look back.

    I did a lot of wrong things in my life and caused a lot of pain to other as well. I was so mad at my mom that I didn't want talk to her.

I was angry and bitter because I needed her to protect and comfort me and she didn't.

Well I learned later that my mom had an illness and she wasn't responsible for taking care of herself or anyone else. They had been planning to take us from our mother. Even when they told her to go and get help they wouldn't take us away from her, their minds were made up then, so even when she did get help they were still set on putting us in foster care. My Aunt found out about it and took us out of the state and gave us to our other Aunt. I didn't want to leave my mom, I felt like she needed someone to love and care for her. I asked myself if I had stayed in Kentucky would I have been sexually abused by my stepdad? And would I have had to go through the abuse with my son's father like I did? Without the pain, there is no praise. All I could do was praise God that my little sisters were in a safe place and out of harms way.

When a person has been hurt by the pains of life. They don't intentionally set out to hurt others. They are just striking out in anger. I am guilty of hurting others because of the pain that I caused them. I am not making excuses but I didn't know any better.

All my life, I saw people cheating on their spouses, so I thought it was okay. So I didn't look for what was right or wrong, I just looked for ways to take care of Jackie and my son. I wanted to give my son everything that I didn't have so I stole, cheated people out of their things and didn't care who got hurt in the process as longs as I was okay. I even slept with men, didn't even care if they were married or not.

But one Sunday at church, I heard the preacher preaching, saying do unto others as you would have them to do unto you. At first, his words didn't have meaning to me, but then over the next few days I heard the voice of my grandmother and all her friends that I had grew up around, saying stuff like this, "Baby if you be good, God sure will take care of you. Baby don't take from others, look to

God to take care of you. He will provide everything you need. Baby be good to all people, whether they have hurt you or not. God will take care of them. Baby don't let things that you have been through turn you into a bitter old woman. But Jackie, be the woman that God wants you to be." When I went to bed that night, I continued to hear their voice, this was back in 1986. I cried out to God to take control of my life. I packed up my things and moved to Bruce, MS. Little did I know is that this would be a whole other set of pains. I was at a crossroad with nowhere to go but Jesus was standing there with me.

I left my footprints in the sand from Prairie to Aberdeen and from Aberdeen to Shannon and from Shannon back to Okolona back to Bruce.

Leaving my footprints in the sand from one place to the other reminded me of the Poem by Author Carolyn Joyce Carty,"Footprints" as she described a man had a dream that he was walking along the beach with the Lord and how his life flashed across the sky and He could see scenes of his life and for each scene he saw two sets of footprints in the sand, one belonged to him and the other to God. The part in the last scene of his life when things got really rough he could only see one set of footprints and this bothered the man because he felt like God had abandoned him. So after questioning God about it leaving him in the most troubled times when he really needed Him, and the Lord explained to him that in the most troubled times, was when He carried him that's why he only saw one set of footprints. In these times in my life is when I found out who JESUS was. He was carrying me because I was unable to walk, reflecting back all I can say is, "Thank You Jesus!"

When I found out who Jesus was, this made a great difference in my life. My life got a lot better. Knowing Him gave me a boldness wanting to let others know who Jesus is!

Jesus is my Savior!

Jesus is my Healer!
Jesus is my Father!
Jesus is my Master!
Jesus is my Teacher!
Jesus is my King!
Jesus is my Lord!
Jesus is my God!
Jesus is my Way!
Jesus is my Truth!
Jesus is my Life!
Jesus is King of Kings and Lord of Lords!

6

Emotional, Physical & Mental Abuse

In 1986, I moved to Bruce to be closer to my father's side of the family. I was still working on getting over the pains I had endured. I just wanted a fresh start. So my first week being there, I found a job and an apartment. Glory to God! He was getting ready to take me to the next level of my life.

Living there, I got to know many people. My spirit was never at rest when I was around some of them, so I stayed out of their way. But there were some that made a huge impact on my life and I will always remember and love them.

I met my grandfather for the first time, but kept my distance from him. I was scared to let him hug me. I shivered whenever he tried. The sexual abuse had taken a toll on me, I was afraid and nervous and didn't want any man touching me. But with my grandfather, Floyd Holland and his wife Jimmie D. Holland, I found a new kind of LOVE. I felt secure and safe around them. I got closer to my grandfather and allowed him to hug me and what a feeling! It felt so good to be loved.

My boyfriend and I moved in together in 1988, having my second son. In December of 1988, we got married and life was so sweet. My mom moved in with us to help with the children. This was the beginning of a new relationship for me and my mother. My new mother-in-law took me under her wings and she became my biggest prayer warrior and my best friend. This woman taught me to look beyond the things that were going on around me and to step out in faith to reach the goal that had been set for me. My husband and I were good, he accepted my first son as his. Peace, joy and happiness in my life all together at one time for the first time! I joined Jackson Chapel Baptist Church and I was ready to serve. I was ready to do whatever was needed in the church.

1991 it hit, our marriage started sliding downhill. I began to look at myself to see what was I doing wrong. I tried talking to my husband and it seems it made things worse. I began to notice when out shopping or just out and about I would see this one lady who I didn't know, would bump into me or she would always roll her eyes at me. It never failed. I opened my mouth to say something but the only thing that came out was, "It's okay, have a good day." I told my husband about it, that every time this lady saw me she made it her business to bump into me or say something under her breath. He said it was all in my head. I prayed and ask God to reveal to me what was going on and to show me how to handle it. The Lord said to me, "Be still and know that I am God. Psalm 46:10. I started praying for this lady and asking God to be merciful to her. My husband did not know this was about to affect his family. Before he could even get a word out of his mouth, I already knew that he was going to say. I felt so betrayed and hurt but I didn't let it get me down. He told me he was leaving to be with this woman because he had fallen in love with her. I told him to have a good life. After this the lady continued to bump into me trying to make a scene but I didn't fall into her trap. I wanted to say something but every time I opened my mouth, the only thing that came out was, "Walk with me Lord."

Not long after our separation, he wanted to come back home. I allowed him to come back, but we only fought. But it was one Sunday evening, I sent him out of my life, but not without the last meal. I got up that morning and fixed all of his favorite foods for his dinner. He sat there and ate until he got full. He told me how good the food was. I was glad that he enjoyed it, I smiled and packed the rest of it for him and I told him to take it with him. I knew in my heart that God had brought me to far up the road for me to fall in that trap. For the first time in my life, I was in a happy place being in a relationship with Jesus.

I remember Martha Nell telling me to find out who Jesus was to me and who I am to Jesus. I found out! He was my sweet resting place. He still is. I found out that he loved me unconditionally and He still does. I found out that I could face all things with Jesus. There is nothing impossible with Him. I remember Martha Nell telling me to learn who the battle really belongs to. The word said, "vengeance is mine," said the Lord.

During this time the Lord was preparing me for a job and I didn't know what it was but I was willing to follow Him, no matter where it led me. Things had gotten so bad with me and my husband that I started dating again. It was not a happy relationship because it was not of God. But later my husband and I tried to rebuild our marriage. I found out that I was pregnant with my third son. I went to my husband and his mom and confessed to the both of them that the baby might not be theirs. At that moment, I knew without a doubt that it was over. But he looked at me and said, "You didn't make that mistake by yourself. If I had not been doing what I was out there doing and been at home there would be no doubt about whose baby it was. In March of 1992 my third son was born. He was the joy and sunshine of my life.

Back when I first begin to tell my story, I told about me slipping and drinking and how it was a problem for me. Well, after I had the baby I started having problems out of my liver and I stayed sick. My husband stayed with me for the better and worse, but not through the sickness and health. But his mother never left my side. One doctor after another for two years straight and after a while I started feeling better and getting around again. My husband wanted to get back together, and I told him that we could be friends but not a couple. We found out that we were better friends.

In 1994, I was diagnosed with cancer in my uterus. After going to different doctors it was decided that I needed surgery because I was losing lots of blood. I ended up having a hysterectomy, it was risky and a long recovery, BUT GOD! In this time, God used it to prepare for the job he had waiting for me.

So one night, after recovering from my surgery I heard a knock at my door, it was a lady from the DHS office. I was like Oh Lord they are getting ready to take my children! I heard the Lord say, "Never fear my child you are ready for your job. My husband and his girlfriend, had a baby. The baby was born sick, she spent the first six months of her life in the hospital in Jackson, MS. The lady at the door said she was told to bring the baby to me and I was going to be her caregiver. I told her that I didn't know anything about this. The Lord said to me, "When you were being pushed around, I was preparing you for my glory!" The lady that was bumping into me was the baby's mom. The other ladies were her friends, trying to pick a fight with me, but that was not part of God's plan for me. The battle was not mine.

God had planned for me to take the baby in and give her what she needed the most and that was LOVE. I came to love that baby like I had given birth to her. Loving this baby brought me and mom even closer together. But she left us in 1996. Baby-girl gained her heavenly wings. 1994-1996, she made a huge impact in our lives. She taught us how to love again.

As I think about it, it could have been real bad, when the lady kept bumping into me, BUT GOD! The Lord brought something good out of that, Miss Tenisha Armstrong 1994-1996. We don't know the plans that God has for us but we have to trust Him because He tells us he has a good, pleasing and perfect plan and will for our life. Jeremiah 29:11.

Look at my husband and I, we fought but through it all, I found peace through the pain. It might sound crazy but it is true. We serve and awesome God.

7

Encouragment and Inspiration

Here are fifteen quotes to encourage and inspire ourselves about the power of letting go of things, people, thoughts and ideals in order to grow and adapt to the present and embrace your future with positivity and happiness.

1. Surrender to what is, let go of what was. Have faith in what will be.

2. In the end, only three things matter.
    a. How much you loved
    b. How gently you lived.
    c How gracefully you let go of things not meant for you

3. Anything that costs you your peace is too expensive. Learn to let go.

4. We must be willing to let go of the life we have planned, so as to have the life that is
>> waiting for us.

5. Let it hurt. Let it heal. Let it go!

6. Just let go. Let go of how you thought your life should be and embrace a life that is trying
>> to work its way into your consciousness.

7. One of the happiest moments in life is when you can find the courage to let go of what you
>> cannot change.

8. Letting go gives us freedom and freedom is the only condition for happiness. If in our heart
>> we still cling to anything such as anger, anxiety or possessions we cannot be free.

9. Whatever comes, let it come. Whatever stays let it stay, whatever goes, let it go!

10. Sometimes letting things go is an act of far greater power than defending or hanging on

11. It is tough to let go of someone you cannot live without, but living with someone who
>> can live without you is much worse.

12. You can live your life angry, bitter or mad at someone or even guilty, not letting go of
>> you own mistakes but you won't receive the good things God has in store.

13. It hurts to let go, but sometimes it hurts more to hold on.

14. If you want to fly in the sky, you need to leave the earth. If you want to move forward,
>> you need to let go of the past that tracked you down.

15. Letting go does not mean you stop caring. It means you stop trying to force others to.

Contentment

As I went through life, I always desired to have everything I didn't have and that kept me very unhappy. It stressed me out, not being able to get what I wanted. Even when I did have the money to get the things that I wanted, there was always someone else who needed something, so I would put what they needed above what I wanted. I found out that all my needs were met.

I learned that there was a difference in being happy and being content . Happiness is the feeling we get when we get what we want by having our desires met.

Contentment, on the other hand, is the feeling of not having the desire to begin with. If you feel content, you're satisfied and happy with what you have at the moment trusting and believing that God will bless you with what you need when you need it.

We deceive ourselves when we measure our happiness or contentment in life by the amount of wealth we possess. When we put our riches at the top of our value system their power, pleasure and security overshadows the eternal value of our relationship with God. We think we will be happy or content when we get riches only to discover that they don't really satisfy and the pleasures fade away.

The true measurement of happiness or contentment is found in God's love and in doing His will. You will find true happiness if you put your relationship with God above earthly riches. God can either deliver us or help us remain steady as we go through trouble and pain. God's protection is best for us when we feel like we are drowning in our troubles, we should reach out and ask God to hold us steady.

In God's care, we are never helpless. God's protection of His people is limitless and can take many forms. If you need protection, look to the Lord. He's all you need! We have not because we ask not!

Contentment is not in what we eat, do or where we live. Contentment is being satisfied in all circumstances of life regardless of whatever. Philippians 4:11-13 Paul tells us that he wasn't saying these things because he's in need, but he has learned to be content in whatever the circumstance. Verse 12, Paul said he knows what it is to be in need and he knew what it was like to have plenty. But Paul says that he has learned the secret of being content in any and every situation, whether well fed or hungry. Whether living in plenty or in want. Then in verse 13, Paul said,"I can do all things through Christ who strengthens me. See, this is the lesson that I had to learn . Once I learned this, the things in my life began to even out. Things that I wanted did not even make sense to me any more.

1Timothy 6:6 But Godliness with contentment is great gain. 7. For we brought nothing into the world and we can take nothing out of it. I had to learn that every conversation was not for me to take part in. I had to learn the difference between unhealthy and healthy relationship. I no longer had a desire to be around people who talked about each other and put each other down. I realized that I had a lot of growing to do. I learned in 1Timothy 6:9 those who want to get rich fall into temptation and a trap and into many foolish and harmful desires that plunge people into ruin and destruction. 10. For the love of money is a root of all kinds of evil. Some people, eager for money, have wondered from the faith and pierced themselves with many griefs.

1Timothy 6:11 being a woman of God, I had to flee from unrighteousness, godliness, faith, love, endurance and gentleness. 12. I had to learn to fight the good fight of faith. And reading Matthew 6:33-34 placed the golden rule in my heart, "But seek ye first His Kingdom and his righteousness and all these things will be given to me as well. 34. Therefore do not worry about tomorrow, for tomorrow will worry about itself. Each day has enough trouble of its own.

BE CONTENT IN GOD'S MERCY AND HIS GRACE AND EVERYTHING WILL BE ALRIGHT!
DEPEND ON GOD NOT MAN!

Proverbs 3:5-6 Lean not to your own understanding but acknowledge Him in everything you do. Remind yourself who you are to God.

Psalm 139:14 We are fearfully and wonderfully made.

Psalm 17:8 We are the apple of our Father's eye.

God loves us so much that He knows how many strands of hair that we have on our head. Luke 12:7

8

So-Called Friends & True Friends

Learning the difference between a so-called friend and a true friend. People come into your life, some for a lifetime and some just for a season and some are just passing through. They come for all different reasons.
Some to lift you up
Some to tear you down.
Some to make you laugh
Some to make you cry
Some to give
Some to take.
A so-called friend will sometimes tell you what you want to hear, just to try to make you feel better. They know you are wrong, but they will urge you to do it anyway. They know what you are doing will cause you more hurt and pain but because of their love for envy they will encourage you to keep going just to give them something to laugh and talk about. As long as they think you have something

and they can get it they will tell you whatever you want to hear. But when you are down they are now here to be found..

    A true friend, will correct you when you are wrong whether you like it or not. If they know that you are getting yourself into some trouble, they will stop you They will always encourage you to walk away from trouble and just pray about it. A true friend will be right there always there by your side. I have found a few good friends in my life that have helped me to grow in many different areas of my life. They always kept me on the right track, and never minded telling me what was on their mind. Whenever I was wrong they would let me know I was wrong. They always encouraged me to grow in the Lord. God's word will never fail, Joshua 21:45 God keeps His word not one of God's good promises have ever failed. Luke 1:37 For the word of God will never fail. These women spoke God's word to me and over me and my life.

    I met a friend back when I was a very young girl and to me she was a model of what a real woman should be. She always told me to always let my yes be yes and my no be no, that it would get me farther along in life. I always wanted to tell her the secret I had in my heart but I was so afraid she would take my mom's side. I wanted to talk to her about what happened to me and also about being grown and taking care of myself. When I would go out with her, drinking was a NO! I liked the way that she dressed, carried and took care of herself. She handled her business. She was a hard worker, I never heard of ask or beg for anything. She taught me, watching her instilled in me to work hard for what I wanted. She always told me that I was a woman and don't ever let anyone tell me anything different. She told me to always hold my head up and always present myself like a lady and to never let anyone treat me different. She always stood for what was right, true and pure. She always told me it's okay if you don't fit in with some people because maybe those are the people that God doesn't want in your life. There are going to be some people that don't want to have anything to do with you and I say it's okay, God has a group for you just ask Him and He will lead them to you.

A true-friend will pray for you when you don't have the strength. They will cry with you, laugh with you, feed you when you are hungry and give you shelter. Speak out on what God say about your life. Be a friend to someone around you. You never know who's in need of a good God fearing friend.

I just want to share with someone who was like me, and thought that no one cared. Just know someone cares and they love you very much. Remember that we have a Great One who sits high and looks low.

God Cares

God Sees

God Knows

God Loved you from the beginning of time.

He knew us before we were formed in our mother's womb. Jeremiah 1:5 before I formed you in the womb I knew you. And He showed us how much He love and care for us, He gave us His only begotten Son, all we have to do is accept Him and believe in Him. Jesus is our one True Friend. There is nothing that we face in life that is too hard for God to handle. Things that were meant to break me, gave me strength to get up and carry on. Always remember that everything that happens in your life is not meant to break you. Ecclesiastes 3:1-8 tells us there is a time for everything and a season for every activity under the heaven 2. A time to be born and a time to die. Ecclesiastes 3:14 tells us that everything God does will endure forever, nothing can be added or nothing taken away. We all will have to stand in front of God one day. So please don't hold anything against anyone that has caused pain in your life.

Even through my pain, I learned to forgive and love those who hurt me. I also learned to ask for forgiveness for those that I have hurt. God wants us to love everyone. We all will have to face the consequences of our own actions. Romans 12:19 Do not avenge ourselves, but leave for God's wrath. God said that vengeance is His and He will repay.

9

Prison Set Me Free

It might sound crazy please just hear me out, going to prison was the best thing that happened to me. I was wild and out of control. But I had already imprisoned myself before setting foot into a physical one. The pain that I was harvesting on the inside of me kept me locked down like I was already in chains. It took going to prison to set me free. It's when I let go of all this pain I was able to enjoy God's healing in my life.

In January 1998, I boarded a bus that took me to Rankin County, Pearl Mississippi. The Judge had sentenced me to ten years. Leaving my children behind was the worst pain I have ever endured in my life. It was far worst than sexual abuse and no one believing me, it was way worst than being hit or choked! It was horrible and I couldn't stop the tears from falling. There were so many thoughts going through my head. Were my kids going to be okay? What if something happened to them or my parents while I'm here locked up? Were they crying and missing me the way I was missing and crying about them? My thoughts consumed me, they begin to eat me alive. What if this? What if that? In the middle of my pity party and officer came and called for us to take our clothes off so that we could be checked. Fear arose in me, and anger over took me. I didn't know what was going on but I did not want to take my clothes off. A woman officer came and took me by the hand, she said to me, "You better stop all of this crying or people are gonna think that you are weak. I then at that moment admitted to her, "I am weak and lost!" Not only did she hear me but God heard me and He, the Lord said to me, "I am your strength, do not be afraid." After getting check in, my name changed fro Jackie R3017. In prison you have a number assigned to you.

While getting processed, I cried out to the Lord, to take control of me and not let me leave the way that I came. I asked the Lord to shape me and mold me into the person that He wanted me to be. I told the Lord I wanted to see things the way He wanted me to see them. I have to admit that I was very hurt, but it was because of the decisions that I had made in my life.

After I was assigned to the unit that I was to spend the rest of my first few month in I decided I was going to stay to myself. I didn't want to be bothered by anyone. I had never in my life experienced something like this, I had to raise the tissue and asks for permission to use the bathroom! Lord there were all kinds of women, just stacked on top of each other. I was like, "Ooooo No, I can't do this!" But the little voice inside of me said, "Yes you can! You can do all things through Christ who strengthens you. Philippians 4:13.

One afternoon, an officer stepped on our Zone and asks for a few people to volunteer to help clean and take the trash out. No one volunteered so she started calling numbers out K005, T1234, Z5678 and R3017 that was my number. "Why me Lord?" I said. "Why not?" ask the Lord. When I walked up to her she told me what she wanted me to do. I looked at her and said , "No I am not doing anything!" So she sent me to the Sergeant's office. I went in there with the same I don't care attitude. I thought I was hard but this Sergeant broke me down. She was Sergeant Bird. I was sitting there rolling my eyes at her and she was sitting there smiling that really made me mad. She introduced herself to me. And I in turn said, "I am R3017", and she smiled and said, " No you are Jackie Bean and you are special." She asked me how long did I have there and I said ten years and I just want to be left alone, I just want to do my time and go home. She looked at me and said, "Bury that attitude and cut out the pity party and get with the program." She explained to me that I could make difference in my life. She told me that it was up to me, I could make my time hard or easy. She told me that I needed to lightened up on myself and stop pretending because she could tell that I was a very loving and kind person. She told me to go to my rack, pray, go to bed and meet her back at her office in the morning when she came to work. When I use the term rack, I'm referring to bed. She told me to think about how I wanted to do my time, the easy way or the hard way.

When she got to work the next day, I was waiting on her with a smile on my face. I was ready to clean her office and take out the trash, but she told me to sit down. She said God has a purpose and a plan for your life, it is up to you to find out what it is but it starts with being obedient. She said obedience is the key to having a right relationship with God.

Over the next few weeks, I used my time to write letters for some of the women who could not write. I even read letters to the ones that couldn't read. I met some Godly women who made a huge impact on my life. As time went by, I started telling the women that MDOC on the back of our shirts meant that we were Mighty Disciples of Christ. I started a relationship with JESUS and that was and still is the best choice that I ever made in my entire life.

A few weeks had passed and I was moved to another building where I was able to get in classes like the Adult and Adolescent Survivors of Abuse January 2000. Step by Step in the New Testament August 2000. I met a lot of women who were wishing that they had a second chance, and then there were those with nothing to lose. I let them know right away, I had a lot to lose and didn't want to give up on life so I chose God..

Some of the women I still keep in touch with even now. I have a desire to one day go in the prison and give my testimony in hopes that it would encourage the women not to give up.

"Someone Knows
Someone Cares
Someone Loves with an everlasting love."

God really blessed me to find favor in the eyes of some of the officers. I even go to witness to some of them.. Not with my words but with my actions. When I arrived there, I was angry, broken, bitter and full of resentment but when I got ready to leave I had a new talk, God was the answer. I had a new walk! God had given me a new outlook on life! I had learned how to let of of the past and run toward the goal that God had set before me. Those old thoughts that had taken over me, were now put to rest by the renewing of my mind. Philippians 4:8 Finally brethren whatever things are true, whatever things are noble, whatever things are just, whatever things are pure, whatever things are lovely whatever things are of good report think on those things.

I came home from prison ins 2004. And when I say God is an on time God, He truly is! I was getting out and they were getting ready to send two of my sons off to training school for boys. When the judge looked up and saw me standing the courtroom He said, "Praise the Lord I am letting them go home with their mother!"

"Tell me what God won't do!" Since then I've been on a roller coaster ride with one of my sons. I came at a time in my life when I had to just remove myself away from my son and trust God to work on him. He was abusive to women and the only thing I could see was him causing me to slide back into a place where I was refusing to go with him! I pray for my son daily but I refuse to travel a road with him that will only lead me back down the same road. I just believe that we have to move out of the way and allow God to do what He has to do to shape them into what He desires. We want to be able to tell them which road to take, and even though they will take their own route, we must pray that they will take the right road.

We can't choose their friends but we can choose to pray for them and pray that they make the right decisions and that God brings the right people into their lives.

10

Pain on Top of Pain

Death hit my family and it seemed like it was no end in sight! I felt like I had lost everything. And then I just gave up. I faced depression, mental and emotional pains. I had fallen and didn't want to get up.

In 2011 I lost two of my family members that were like sisters and brothers to me. It was so hard. When my cousin died, the one that was like a sister to me the only thing I had left was to try and be a comfort to her mother, but for some reason she pulled away from me, she refused to deal with me and that added insult to injury. It went even deeper. My heart hurt. Even though she treated me that way, I still tried to be there for her. I was pushed out again and felt even more worse. My cousin and I were very close. When I moved to Bruce, she moved there as well. We grew up together, from little girls to grown women, we were always there for each other. She died and I felt lost. I prayed and asked God to reveal to me what was gong on with my Aunt, why is she treating me like this? Found out, she was pushing me away because of some money she thought that I had taken from her daughter and my cousin before she died.

Someone told her that I had beat her out of some money. This was not true. I will give before, I take. The money was mine, I had received my last check. And my cousin did receive a check as well, but I took her to pay all her bills and Christmas shopping for her kids. I told all this to my aunt and children but they didn't believe me. I didn't argue with them. I received a phone call to come to the hospital, on my way I just asked the Lord to work it out. The call was about my dad, they had put him in the hospital.

Again at my aunt's the next day, just wanted to be support and wanted to be loved back, after finding out that my daddy had been hospitalized I told my aunt about my dad and that he wasn't doing good, but they didn't want to hear about that, they started talking about the money that I had spent. Again, heartbroken. I had just lost my cousin, sister, best friend all in one person and now the doctors saying I might lose my daddy. He was in his last stage of lung cancer and all they wanted to talk about was money. On December 24, 2011, we buried my cousin and I had to get back to the hospital so I didn't get to my aunt's house. Everyone was saying I was running because I knew that I was wrong. We can't stop people from talking but we are blessed to have a Father that sits high and looks low, and He knows everything that is going on.

On Christmas 2011, one of my cousins called me and he needed to talk to me, so I left the hospital and went to my aunt's house and he said I don't know what you did with my sister's money, but we need it. We got to buy her a tombstone and she left two small kids to take care of. I called his name and told him, "I promise you I did not take any of her money. She spent her money paying bills and Christmas shopping for her kids. He questioned me about paying my van off, as I told him I had my own money. I also had a letter to prove where the money came from but I didn't feel l I ha to prove anything. I was hurting, I needed a hug, love and all I got was hate because of a lie. I didn't have time for this I needed to be with my daddy.

January 5, 2012, my daddy gained his heavenly wings. I was dealing with so much, I just wanted to be left alone. Depression had set in, I didn't want company. I didn't want to talk, no one believed what I had to say anyway. BUT it was God that gave me the peace and comfort that I was needing. He never left my side. I later got a call from my aunt, she wanted me to know that she was heartbroken about my dad. I assured her everything would be okay, to just trusts God.

God worked everything out, even in the midst of the storm. The truth about my cousin's money came out and my aunt found out that I had been telling the truth all along. She did apologize to me but the hurt I was dealing with was not even explainable. I bought my cousin a tombstone, not because I took her money, but because I loved her. And love rules over all.

February 20, 2012, I lost my mother and I am still lost without her. All these different emotions came rushing over me. My mama, my mother, my best friend, my everything even one of my heartbeats, was now gone. She had left me all by myself. There was no one to ease the pain, no words that could be said. I had a whole house full of people and through the pain all I saw was Jesus. I could hear people in the background but I could not understand anything that they were saying. The only voice that I heard was JESUS, saying, "Everything is going to be alright with me and I'll stay with you!' My peace was in Jesus, my comfort was in Jesus and my strength was in Jesus. I stood through it all. I know we can handle it with Jesus because He an do the impossible. Whatever the pain is, it's not too hard for God.

11

Can't Do it Alone

The things we face trying to do things ourselves. Getting upset about our problems never changes them. It is impossible to live a trouble free life, but it is possible to live a faith-filled life. 1Corinthians 12:9, God's strength is made perfect in our weakness. 1 Corinthians 10:13, God promises to never allow more than what we can bear. Romans 8:35 reminds us that no matter how difficult life is God loves us.

During difficult times we've got to avoid thinking the worst and start to think how God wants us to think. In 2012 I almost broke! I did bend but I didn't break! God kept me here! June 30, 2012 I found a glimpse of the rainbow. I found happiness and rain with it and ran straight into a brick wall, a road block even the Great Wall of China. I forgot that Jesus was supposed to take the lead. I got married and it didn't take me long to find out that in order for us to make it in this marriage, there was going to have to be Jesus. Abuse I endured because no one listened, no one believed that he would do that. The Lord told me to stand still this battle was His. Lies were told on me to one of his family members and that person refuses to speak to me because of the lie. But God said that HE would reveal the truth, just stand still and know that I am God. God is using me to show my husband that He is God and one day everyone will bow. We had a situation in our home involving him pulling a gun on me because of something that he thought I said. So maybe you think I'm crazy but I had him put in jail, I took a stand a bold stand for God. Everyone that doubted what I was saying before, still didn't believe until he started doing the same things to them. And the same people that didn't believe me now realized that they didn't know him the way they thought they did.

God wants us to know HIM. He will take a nobody to tell anybody about somebody who can save us all. Even though we still have a long ways to go, I can truly say that things are not where they need to be but they are a long ways from where they were. I don't depend on my husband. I depend on God because a long time ago I would have walked away, but God let me know it was not time yet.

God places people in my life to help me and I have lost so many of them but He lets me know He is with me until the end of times. God is always the answer.

12

Dealing with Pain through God's Word

Enjoying life is a choice. I could have chosen to let the pain in my life destroy and consume me but I chose God and I chose life. My life is not an easy one and I don't wish the road that I've traveled on anyone. I am beginning to look at life in a different way and it is my heart's desire for everyone to experience the love that God has for them. Although we don't always have the power to change the things going on in our lives, we do have the power to choose a faith filled life, living on the promises of God. Romans 8:28 says All things are working for our good, let's watch God work these things out in our lives.

Enjoying this life begins with our THOUGHTS, what do we choose to think? If we choose to happy hope-filled thoughts based on God's word we will feel happier. When we choose the positive and expect and believe God to do great things it releases joy into our lives and we don't have time to focus on the pains. Nothing good comes from thinking sour, critical and negative thoughts, but something good always comes when we think according to God's plan for our lives.

Enjoying this life begins with the thoughts we choose to think. Deuteronomy 30:19 I call heaven and earth to record this day against you that I have set before you life and death, blessings and curses; therefore choose life, that both you and your seed made live.

In order for me to get passed my pain, I first had to start thinking about myself. God thinks that I am wonderful and it's important that I think the same way about myself. So I had to forget about the past and move on toward my future. Philippians 3:13 even after God forgiven us we continue to hold on to unforgiveness and that leads us down a road called no where.

The pain is real and so is God's grace and mercy. I had to realize that I was not walking alone. God was always with me. Through my cloudy eyes and stormy heart. I just could not see Him but I could feel Him.

Just to Say Thanks

I want to send a shout out to my Grace Family:
Pastor Jermal Boddie, Sr., Minister Amy, Evangelist Linda, Tangi, Sonya and Deacon Arthur

My Prayer Warriors:
Martha N.Bean, Charlotee McHenry, Amy Deanes, Lori Pierce Dreux

www.ingramcontent.com/pod-product-compliance
Lightning Source LLC
Chambersburg PA
CBHW052126110526
44592CB00013B/1774